FCHW

FAITH, CONSISTENCY & HARD WORK

I truly thank you for
taking a chance on me.
Blessings! -JB

FCHW—Faith, Consistency & Hard Work

ISBN-13 978-0-9895965-4-1

Just Published by Restore Me Org.
restoremeorg@gmail.com

FCHW

FAITH, CONSISTENCY & HARD WORK

SPOKEN REASONS

RESTOREME

I remember waking up every morning to walk to school... Every morning to catch the bus to work... Now every morning I wake up doing whatever and catching planes... May not seem like much to you, but I'm grateful... There is no official day when you "Make it"... You'll just be living and will be so wrapped up into your dream that you'd forget where you are at the moment. Thank God for everything... You'll never know how far you will get if you never spend time flexing your muscles for growth!! #FCHW #TBPG

Note to the reader,

What you are about to read is raw and uncut. It was also written at a time when Spoken Reasons was very young. The goal was to keep it as pure as possible to its original form in order to offer you a genuine piece of Spoken Reasons. Since writing these as a teenager, Spoken Reasons has experienced tremendous growth as an entertainer and a man. Thank you for your support, and growing with us.

— #FCHW Team

Somebody

19 years old, born and raised in Bradenton Florida, right below Tampa, and I am somebody...

Raised up by two dynamic females, my mamma and grandma, and I was always told that I am somebody.

Around age 3 I was left by somebody, lets just say that the somebody is the same reason why I'm stuck with my last name right now.

Left because he was a ... "sigh"

but at age 4 my momma found that real somebody.

The type of somebody that already had finish raising kids, but had one extra room left for that fatherless kid.

And he said to me "boy you are somebody."

He told me to put down the video game remote and made me go outside and shoot my 1st hoop and swing my 1st bat, because he wanted to find the somebody that I was.

"Hey daddy!! Can you teach me how to fish?"

And he taught me how to fish. I remember when we used to go fishing. His name was "right hook" and my name was "bait"

And while we were fishing he said "Son, I may not be your real daddy but God put me in this world to grab you as my bait and right hook you on my hook, because you gone be somebody one day."

And I felt like a somebody.

Until 3rd grade, February 1998 when I was 10, I loss the man that told me I was gone be a somebody one day.

And I will never forget when I 1st saw you just laying there, while my uncle was singing "here at the cross" I was saying, "Damn I'm a nobody."

And its like my mamma read my mind and she said "Son you gone be somebody."

And from there on I loss it, running wild, acting wild, fucking up in school.

And I remember when I was in 4th grade my teacher said, "You keep making grades like this and you won't make it out of school."

But bitch I'm somebody, and I got written up for calling that lady a bitch...

And the referral read, "John called me a bitch."

And my mamma said, "why you called her that?"

Because you, grandma, and daddy said I'm somebody and that's why I called her a bitch because the bitch couldn't see clear enough that I am somebody.

From 4th grade to 12th grade I almost failed every single grade in school, but I graduated. I graduated because I was told I was somebody and I wanted to do it for me and the people that said I am somebody.

So watchu gone do with yo life?

SOMEBODY

I'm moving to Orlando to start a new life. I got to get up out of this place because it aint nothing here for me.

I'm gonna go to Valencia to get my AA degree, and after that I might just transfer to UCF because I wanna pledge in a fraternity and become a black greek.

But deep down inside, college just aint for me.

I feel like I'm wasting my time.

After all, I don't need college, my major don't require college anyway, I'm just gonna go to police academy to become a correctional officer to work round lil' kids.

"You dropping out of school?" Yeah, I'm going to police academy in the summer to become a correctional officer.

Man you aint shit if you drop out of school!!!

You aint nothing but a god damn fool!!

And I took it and remembered what my mamma said to me "Son, whatever you do as long as you do something good with your life, I won't complain."

I mean, my daddy dropped out of school, he was a somebody.
My mamma dropped out of school, she somebody.
My grandma dropped out of school, she somebody.
I aint tryna follow they footsteps but I know whats best for me and I am somebody.

Like I said before you a fool for dropping out of school, you aint gone be shit with yo life without a degree.

Hold up...so you telling me that I aint shit if I don't stay in school and get my degree?

So I got to have a bachelors, a masters, and a PHD?

Just to prove the world that aint shit wrong with me?

I'm saved, I know the plans and goals I got set in my life, so just because I aint in college that make me a aint shit nigga?

Fuck that, I am somebody, just because you got yo degree, don't make you any more or less than me...

So you stay in school and get yo bachelors, masters, and PHD because you aint shit.

Just because you got yo bachelors, masters, and PHD don't mean nothing.

I'm somebody without them degrees and you aint shit because I bet you aint settle for yo G.O.D.

Now tell me I aint somebody...

Do what's best for you, and I'm gone do what's best for me...

Why? Because I am somebody!!

My Little Town

It hurts me, it hurts me everyday to look back and see what's going on in my little town.

My town is small and everybody knows each other.

So small that every homeboy and home girl you got is related to each other.

So small that folks don't know they cousins from they brothers.

You see as a lil boy my mamma raised me up as a single mother all my life basically.

But thank God I had a father figure for 5 years to somewhat see what the good roads there were for me in the future.

I seen a lot in my 19 years, prolly seen more than half of you in your 30's could ever see.

I remember them days when my mamma used to drop me off to my grandma house and my elementary school was 30 min away, walked there and back every single day.

I even remember when walking from school It was always somebody saying,"Ima kick yo ass when we get out",even though we aint know the meaning of cussing then anyway.

I could also remember the same kids that got sent to the office everyday for doing something stupid.

Everyday after school they used to fight, then I became the person in some of those fights.

Fighting off kids that said they aint like you cause you said "yo mamma" at the lunch table when they started talking bout yours in the 1st place.

Scared for that bell to ring after school cause these lil jokers was gone jump me.

But as soon as that bell rang I was gone. It took 30 mins to walk from my grandma house and back, and sometimes I got there in 12.

Going in the house breathing all hard, "boy you got here kinda fast".

"Yea I know", and my mamma used to get there before me sometimes for her lunch break.

Boy, who you running from? Nobody. Boy lemme tell you something, whoever you running from you show them who da big bad wolf is.

When I was in school I aint play that mess, I was quiet but if they wanted to step up

They shol got it.

Whoever you running from, fight em, and you better whoop they ass.

And I fought, fought every single day almost until the whole school wanted to jump me.

But that was my childhood in my little town.

Now I can't fight physical no more because that was the lil league, now this is the big league, I thought that was reality, but this mess here is reality.

I'm talking about reality from middle school on up.

"You can't fight physical no more" mamma said, "it got too bad out here to be doing all that, you can't do nothing in this little town that's physical no more."

You can't even have physical sex cause the town was so small that 30% of my high school had aids. Now just imagine the town.

I can't even have a homeboy to play ball with no more, because if you fouled em too hard he would wouldn't get physical with you, he would get mental and follow his mental instructions and blast you.

Even my mother thinks mental and owns rifles in her closet. When I used to come home late she used to tell me to call before I got there because if I dared walk in the house. She said "I wont hesitate"

You see in all these big cities like Miami, Atlanta, LA., they are well known because of they have something good in it.

Trust me, you think they would be saying these cities on tv if it wasn't nothing good coming out of it? Please.

In my little town ball players are well known from there, but when they get to college and pros the law recruits them as inmates.

They say the smallest thing could be the ugliest thing, well my town to me is the ugliest thing.

I've seen pregnant teachers lose they baby from an angry black fist.

Seen naked babies in the hood running in the road like the stray dogs with no collar looking for a home.

And people think cause you move out the hood everything supposed to get better. You still got connects. You still got the 411. You still got somebody in the hood who you visit and you still got somebody that wanna kill you.

Living in the suburbs I still got da 411 on people that I grew up with getting shot, and killed over money.

Still had brothers running round cause they folks kicked em out the house and wanted to spend a night...cause my side of the grass was green while theirs is brown.

Still visited folks that I grew up with since elementary school, that got killed in my little town.

You see in my little town, everybody had a dirt bike. If you had a dirt bike you had it made.

I aint never had a dirt bike cause my mamma realize that dirt bikes is a real hype in the hood and she wanted to keep my nose in Christ.

But my homeboy had a bike. 15 years old I thought he had it made, but he didn't make it when the truck driver ran the stop sign and knocked em off the bike leaving him on the ground dazed.

Laying there with his body on one side and the bike on the other, tryna push himself up, the driver aint know what he had hit so he put the truck in reverse, and ran him over again.

Crushing his head, leaving nothing but a pool a blood with every part of the face left on the road in every which way.

This is what I saw in my little town.

When you look folks dead in the face as a child in your classroom full of 30, not knowing that 10 years from now, you can reflect on the yearbook and say nothing but one word "DAMN".

Seen girls in classrooms that you swear was bad back in the day, but she done cut her hair off, got tatted up, changed her clothes and turned gay.

Seen girls that get pregnant at age 15 tryna tell they baby what to do and beating cussing and slapping'em like they dumb. When you still a baby yourself too.

Seen dudes that was soft as hell in school. Found the wrong click to hang with, sold drugs and got girls but the next day you were though.

Seen ghetto white boys that grew up round a black society, pulling every black girl around and made mixed babies, It aint bout your color, Its all about watchu come up around.

Got drunk cousins and uncles riding round on bikes high off of crack bout to rob my mamma at church coming home from choir rehearsal not knowing that was they own folks.

Got a step brother that used to beat me up, and lie to daddy and told'em I was the one that did it, and got 2 beatings.

Ran away from home, got locked up, and when daddy died he wasn't there for the meeting.

Got released 6 years later and the nigga decided to mess with the wrong one. Got caught up molesting a 13 year old girl and aint getting out till 2021.

This is what I saw in my small town.

When you see everybody that did or didn't graduate get stuck in that troubled system, because they don't know any better.

They wont leave cause that's what they call home, If that's where you feel comfortable at why leave

But let me tell you something, all things that you call home don't make you feel at home and that's what I seen.

That's why I left that lil small town.

I left because I was down, and God picked me up turned me around, and placed my feet in another location on a solid ground.

Then I found myself, then I found my crown, I found my real purpose for me being around.

All because I left that lil small troubled town.

I found a better connection with God, I found knowledge, and the knowledge of my mind went to my heart and my heart felt that it needed to be spoken, Then I found spoken word.

And I thank God for putting my life in that lil small town. because you got to make it past the darkness to see the light.Otherwise you will never see the light when its in your face.

If you thought that was all of it, that wasn't even half of it. I'm not gone tell you everything, I gotta have something to hold on to.

The rest that I hold on to wont get passed around, dats between me and my little town.

Hired

Employers/boss; person that hires people to do work

Ladies your role in the world is to hire the right brother on board, and seek honesty, loyalty, and all the other things you think will make him right for your foundation...

Employee/worker; person who works for a company or an individual

Fellas, we must understand that being an employee is something that is earned...And we must understand that the ladies aint hire us on board for no apparent reason...It was something in yo black ass that they liked...and that's why you passed the interview process over the other 15 dudes that tried to get on board with her...treat that employer with all respect as if you were respecting yo mamma...

Tyrone was hired by Becky after she fired 3 of her last employees she thought she trusted a year ago

Unemployed as he was...The brother couldn't last long without a job...so he took his happy ass to the unemployment office to get a fast employment from his club...

Dancing and grinding on all these different employers in the club... He still couldn't find the right job for that shit...

Then his senses told him to turn around...BAM!! That's the job that he wanted to work for...I mean this job looked like it had benefits for being a good cook, good character, good quality...hell...it had everything he was looking for...

Becky wasn't seeing nothing good so she decided to leave...

Is she leaving...Wait!!! Hold up...

"nigga what's wrong with you?"

Man look at that bad woman over there...she got help wanted written all over her...

Man you aint gone get that job...

I bet you I will...I'm dressed right, smelling right...watch this...

Excuse me are you accepting applications?

I don't have applications... my niggas have to be prepared with resumes...

Shit, I got that too...

Well lets see it...

26 years old, Orlando born and raised, graduated with a PHD, working 2 jobs, and baby mamma...don't believe in it...

You are hired!!! Here's my number...just give me a call anytime...I'll be available...

But what she don't know is that you lied on your resume trying to make it sound good

Taking her out on a date and your former boss is in the place right along with your former kids that you don't take care of...

Ooo so I see you can pull out some cash and take this ho out to eat but you cant pull out 2 dollars for yo kids...

Hold up I thought you aint have no baby mamma?

Man she crazy...

Now she done hopped up and left...you another unemployed nigga once again...and aint getting no luck playing lovers and friends...

Fellas we must step up and learn to keep our good jobs...our good women...because good jobs are hard to come across to...

So if you pass yo interview and that boss lady likes you...satisfy her with all that is needed...

Remember...not all bosses will put up with yo shit and keep firing and hiring yo ass...

So ladies I crown you the crown of being in charge...and before I go... make sure that yo workers stay on track... if yo employee is slipping then write that nigga up with a lesson to teach...And don't give' em the pussy for 3 weeks...

Nonsense

Go to work and school/

Go to work and school/

Throw away the dream and the plans you had set/

All because of a 3 letter word....... SEX/

How old are you, look at you, what can you do?/15 fool, don't look at me look at you...... After I have this child I'm going back to school/

Scared to walk home to your folks and break the news.

Crying and what not....don't know what to say because they had high expectations of you/

Mamma...Daddy...... I'm (sniff, sniff) I'm pregnant....(father) by who?/

By the 20 year old man who I met after school/

Now daddy thinking...I'm gone kill this dude/

Already pregnant now how can he enforce the rules/

Cant whoop your ass...because the special force will be after his ass/

Got him thinking bout all the mistakes he committed in the past/

Wishing that the dream he heard from your mouth would disappear/

He said...Go to work and school/

Go to work and school/

And don't you bring that nigga over here/

Mamma breaking out in tears/Never thinking that her little girl would grow up so fast in 15 years/

It's not you I'm mad at it's me/

At age 16 I set myself free.

Ran away from home because you grand daddy was abusing me/ Move in with your aunt ruby down in 13th/Then met the little boy across the street/

Same age as I was...We shared our first kiss up under the tree/

And then months later we both felt grown and converted kissing to taking off draws and panties/

Then after draws and panties....here came the baby planning/Scared to tell my folks too/Because they had high expectations of me like I do of you/

Mamma didn't say much when I broke the news/But grand daddy...I had to tell him over the phone to break the news/

He said....Go to work and school/Go to work and school/

And I did so...... dedicated my all my time to open doors/

Not for me.... The door wasn't mine...It was yours/

Now you in the same position I was in 16 years ago...and now its your turn to dedicate/Dedicate your mind, heart, body, and soul...And use God's words to meditate/

NONSENSE

The reason why your father is so mad is because he was the little boy
on 13th/

Lost all his childhood times...because he was focused on you and me/

The little girl took the spoken words from her mother in
consideration/

Sitting down thinking....how she gone make it/

Losing my dreams? My childhood times? My socializing times?/

Hell nah...... Its abortion time/

I'm not ready...I know I'm not ready...

Not ready to go 9 months into labor/Not ready to start having kids
like the flav in front of the flavor/

Not ready to have a baby cause if it cry.... I know I'm gone shake em/

I guess I should of thought about all of that when I laid in the bed/
And let that old dude crack open my crab legs/

Enough is said......

Go to school and work/

Go to school and work/

That's all that matter

Go to school and work/

Go to school and work/

I'm not heartless, I just learned how to use my heart-less!

M.O.E.

Money power and respect...hell yea...that's a true quote right there!!

The money can get you things that you never thought of having in your life...it makes the world turn around!!

The power is the authority for me to make a lot of things happen with the snap of a finger...Just like Suddam Hussein and the Shug Knight...them niggaz had the power!!

Respect...That's just something around society letting you know that you aint shit from the being with..." I don't know you dude...so you got to pay yo dues in order to get through!!"

But notice most thugs got the whole game twisted... M.O.E. is what you see tatted across they stomach...

It stands for money over everything...

And living off of that quote right there will get you messed up!!

You see it every day in the world today performed by thugs...

Let me take my behind to the club...what do I hear? D.j. saying " if you over a stack in a pockets putcha hands up"

Thugs will be quick to raise they hands...its 45 thugs in the club... and its only 2 chunking money in the air...while you got stank chicken heads fighting over the money like porch monkeys...

Everybody is hungry...everybody wants money...

But your money is over everything...

Which means that your money comes 1st...and all the other
bullshit later...

Recruited that 17 year old boy that came up to you needing to make
quick money....because he cant get a job at mcdonalds.... And
mamma working 2 jobs with 5 kids...and they can't keep the lights
on for shit!!

So you gave'em 5 dime bags just to start em off with...

He goes to school the next day and makes his 1st sale...sold one dime
bag to a white boy that things weren't going so well!!

But hours later after the bell...the police confiscated all the drugs
and took the lil boy to jail...

5 days later...charges get dropped...and the lil boy is free...

But lets not forget that your quote is M.O.E...

Where's the rest of the bags that I gave you? Where's my money?
The police took it...

Alright I understand...you're free to go...but you don't wanna kill
him...you wanna kill the one he needs the most...

Click clack power...killed the mother of the 5 kids...because its
M.O.E.

I don't give a damn bout you or your family...yall aint nothing to me....

I'm gone let these niggaz know that my money is valuable to me...

M.O.E.

With me having money nobody can fuck with me... because I got money...the H.O.E's wanna fuck with me... but I wont throw em the dick because the only one that earns my dick is M.O.E.

But it is one that can fuck with you...and that's the police...

Buy all the guns other things that you gone need... but they got k-9's and swat teams... and plus your money is outnumbered by the government cheese....

Get on your knees before we pop 100 seeds in your chest and color the grass red from what you've bled before when the grass was green...

One year later you serving a life sentence...you one less nigga taking out the street and was found guilty of plea!!

Got locked up because you called yourself Mr. M.O.E...

Mr. Money over everything...

But your family, preacher, friends, and teachers called you Mr. J.O.E...

Because you loss your money.,. and chose Jail over everything!!

Knowledge is too accessible & free in this world to be dumb. If u never make it in life, u only have yourself to blame.

Aint No Friends

Coming up...Grandma always made a name for something or somebody... & coming up...Grandma said..."aint no friends"

& errtime I say the word "friend" she would always say "aint no friends" and for a while one... One day I had to think about it...–

Best friends... Buddy buddy... Sidekicks... And home G's 4 life... Ride or die... You fight I fight... In order to get to him or her... You gone have to get through me...

You know I gotcha bruh... You know I gotcha girl...

Some even rob, steal and kill for these so called friends... But hold up... Let me break it down to you...

Grandma lived 15 mins away & since grandma said "aint no friends" I saved a lil bit a money and built her a house, went there on a Sunday afternoon after church, grabbed her by her hand, placed her in that new house and said...

Grandma... This is your new home... & since you make a name for everything Ima need you to name this house... I name this house "watch who"

I cant finish the name so bring some people that's having some friendly issues and I'll finish naming the house...

And for a moment it sounded kinda weird... So I went back home watched T.V... & saw 2 girls pulling each others hair... Pushed pause on the televisions and said... Why are yall fighting?

& one said because this trick stole my man... Well look like to me you need to whoop her behind... So I pressed play back on the remote... And she was her giving homegirl the ass whooping of a lifetime...

So I pushed pause aagin... & she said... Why did you stop us? I said because, & put my arms through da t.v & pulled em out & said... Yall need to come with me...

Took them to grandma at the "watch who" house & grandma said... What brings y'all here? Cause this trick stole my man... Ok... I'm gone name you 2 girls " You & Accept"

J.B... go ahead & leave the house... I'll take care these 2... Go bring me some more...

So I went on campus to UCF... To perform my spoken word & saw 2 frat brothers fighting like lil girls in the hallway... broke it up & said "why are yall fighting"

& one said..."because I left this man in my house & he stole my money" Well look like you need to whoop his behind then... And got into a referee suit & said round 2 fight... And they fought... And he was giving homeboy the ass whooping of his lifetime...

& I'm like watch the head, watch the low blow, watch the kidneys, don't bite his ear off... & broke it up again & he said... "Why did you stop us?" Because...

So I grabbed them 2 frat brothers, threw them in the backseat of my car & drove them all the way back to Brandenton FL, to grandma @ the "watch who" house... & Grandma said... "What brings yall here"

Man because... This man stole my money, & I thought I trusted him...Ok... I'm gone name you 2 boys "In & Your"

But J.B. this time don't leave the house because you need some schooling too... Your name aint J.B. not more... You name is "life"... now stand next to these 4 and listen...

You & Accept... come here... You 2 have been friends for 2 years & know everything about 1 another... Told each other things that will break you both down if you were to tell another person...

So you said that was your friend huh? Just handed them everything that you had his behind the wall in your life and when something came up... you thought you built that trust... but they ran with it...

You let them kick down that wall and exposed them to some things that you wouldn't even tell your own mother...

Like let them kick down that wall of security that you smoke weed, kicked down that wall of security that you accept money to drop on your knees.

Kicked down that wall of security of how many people you slept with, kicked down that wall of security when you trust them with your credit card... Now ima need for you 2 to be quiet and still...

come up here...Now the thing about you 2 is that your fraternal brothers... And I can understand that you 2 are more than just friends... because yall built that brotherly love...

But don't get it twisted...I'm talking about sorority sisters too... Calling each other sisters & I can understand that too...

Hell anybody that hang around each other long enough... They start calling each other brothers and sisters... Brother and sister from another mother... Start treating each them like they really your own blood...

Well whether you like it or not for the people that do this... don't get a pen & paper to write this down... Get a tape recorder... cause after I'm finish play it over and over until your brain creates a general habit...

Because if you do have a brother or sister at home... Just get this... In the beginning there was a man & a woman... & that man & woman fell for each other & had you & your peanut headed brothers & sisters which created a family...

& in that family holds a wall of security of undying love for another, trust, & things that you can spit out to one another... You all are 1...

But I also understand that if you have a brother or a sister that you cant always tell your parents everything...So you cover for one another...Because that's your brother... that's your sister... You suppose to go all out for them...

But why is it that you can hand out so much information to your friends that you call a brother & so call a sister & be willing to do & willing to die for them more than you would for your own damn brother & sisters?

But he or she has been my friend for 8 years... But lets look at this... This person has been your brother & sister all your life!!

Now ima need for you 2 be quiet and still... "Life" come up here... Now I told you at the beginning that it aint no friends... And you bought me... You, Accept, In, & your into this house...

And you wanna know why I named you life... Because some friends are not there every situation & heartbeat of your life...

& I'm not gone say "aint no friends" no more... because it is some true friends out there...

But WATCH WHO YOU ACCEPT IN YOUR LIFE!!

You can plan as much as you want, but always remember that God has the ultimate plans. Just play your role, and he will cover you!

Kelly

Don't worry bout nothing because I'm gone do you better than that last man you had laying round... Just close your eyes and trust me... Because your life is about to change in 5,4,3,2,1...

How you doing whats your name? Kelly...Kelly where you from? And how many kids do you have? I'm from new york and got 3 kids at home without a father...

But before you call yourself trying to hit on me... I'm gonna tell you straight up... I'm looking for a man that can father my kids & comfort me... And if you cant take that then leave...

Kelly don't even worry... I'm a music producer, Allow me to bring home the worm and feed you and your kids mouths with the blessings that no man has ever done before...

All I need for you to do is fast forward to whenever you're comfortable... and tell me you love me and I'll go from there...

Malcom... I appreciate all the things you've been doing for me and my kids... Giving us clothes... taking us out the hood... being the man I've been dying to have... And I think I've found him... I love you...

Kelly that's all I needed to hear from you... Now fast forward 2 weeks from now... Kids get ya mamma and tell her to come to the kitchen for a surprise...

Mamma come in the kitchen look what it is... a birthday cake... 27 birthday candles for you blow out... Go ahead Kelly... Close ya eyes, make your wish, but don't blow out the candles and open your eyes until I tell you to.

Ok, you made your wish? Yea!! Now open ya eyes...Kelly will you marry me on your 27th birthday? Yes!! Ok... Now blow out the candles and fast forward 3 months from now & lets get married, quit your job & move into the 15 bedroom house because we are one!! But before we do that... Let me sex you on this honeymoon!!

Stare each other in the eyes for 10 seconds, ease up our physical defense, picture the love we built upon each other and attach like love bugs for those 2 hours... Cause if you fast forward 9 months from now... This sex delivered us our 1st child!!

Now I'm a step father of 3, biological father of 1, and a husband of 1... While I recorded you giving birth to my 1st child...I though I was a tough guy but I fainted right before my son's foot was exposed to the world...

And the nurses woke me up... Picked up the camera and recorded you holding our child and I leaned over... Kissed my son on the forehead... Then just admired how sexy you looked without make up- and the painful after effects of you giving birth...

And leaned over to kiss your soft lips... And that kiss carried more emotions than 5 females sitting together tearing up popping popcorn over the movie love and basketball!!

Now fast forward this kiss to feb. 14th... Valentines day... you were upset because you thought I forgot your gift... But I told you to your car and press play on the cd player and listen to it...

It was a poem that I recorded and placed in the car for you to listen to... And the poem went like this...

"Kelly you are my love... And I love it when you are around me...

I'll take you to around the world to China, Jamaican, Canada, and Africa with me...

But if something comes up and you cant make it to be beside me on those trips... Ill pull a string of your hair... Place it in my pockets just to make sure a piece of you will always be with me!!"

And you thought it was cute... And for your return you cooked me the best woman-made soul food meal there was... Cause you knew what food to a man's heart could do...

Came up behind me with your arms over my shoulders folded around my chest while I was taking a bite of that friend chicken... And whispered in my ears and said I'm here for you... I will always be here for you!!

But fast forward a year from now... And I'm sitting right here alone saying that I wasn't there fore you... cause on a hard day of work 2 o'clock in the morning... I found myself undressing one of my singers...

And was attached the same exact way you and I were on our honeymoon making love but without the love inserted in this sex because what we were doing was called love making... but this was called fucking... because I was fucking around on my wide and throwing away all the vows I stood before God and promised...& you left me...

And the worst part about it that this story was fast forward another 9 months from now & this sex delivered me my 1st baby mamma and my 2nd child... But Kelly you are not labeled baby mamma in my book... You are the mother of my child...

I didn't even know whether to cry or get mad & kill myself... But I did end up killing myself... Killing myself away from you and my kids as I watched you dress them, packed your bags & haul off in a cab...

Now I'm stuck with a 2nd class baby & a woman I don't want nothing to do with.

Not even used to seeing this house empty... Because you were right here in this house every time I came from work just curious to find out how my day went... So you could know which role to play like a real wife in proverbs 31, 10-31...

And you not being here made me label your name every day and month on my calendar with an "X" next to it... Meaning that you were absent too many times in my life like kinds in a classroom!!

Monday- Sun- Kelly absent

Jan–July- Kelly absent...

But fast forward to your birthday which was August 19th...I decided to call your phone... & you picked up... & I said before you decide 2 make up your mind just put me in the shoes of Avant and give me 4 mins to say what I got to say...

Baby I'm sorry for hurting you... But she sat silent on the phone like none of my deepest offers I was willing to give wont do...

Like standing in the middle of the road with a "Kelly I want you back" T-shirt on wont do...

Having you slap me in the face for every teardrop I caused you wont do...

Like me having Ruben Studdard knock on your door and sing I'm sorry for my 2008 with 3 puppies with words... I love you around they neck... Wont do... To get me back with you...

That's not good enough... she said... you got 2 mins left...

Kelly what do you want me to do? She said spill your heart like you've never done before and after that I'll think about it... You got 1:45 seconds left...

I said Kelly... I was 21 when we 1st met and you were 27... I knew that bringing you into my life would be like brand new car in good condition... I would drive you around across the country with you as a passenger...

And when that car broke down. That young car aint wanna act right... and that point of my life with me cheating on you... was called being young and dumb...

And you left because that car wasn't gonna drive our love any further... So you went to the back of the car, grabbed the kids & walked back to your destination & left.

The second you left I was in darkness looking for a bright light... Matured up quickly as a man & found some jumper cables... And jumped that car with my last sweat just so it could act right...

And drove that car all the way back just to find you... And here I am...

So what do I have to do? I drove all the way back not worrying over gases prices just to be with you... Again...

And if I had powers I would place you on hold... Drop this cell phone on the floor... Spin around 3 times and dive head 1st into the phone... Come out of your ear piece of your phone...

Stand in front of your face, get on my knees... And say...

I want you to be with me... And girl if you thought I was treating you good before troubles.... Well then your wrong...

Cause I was only giving you 40% which means I wasn't even giving you half of me...

But if you accept me back in your life and marry me again I/m gone give you 99.9999% of me... But I'll die tryna give you that .01% just to make it 100% everyday but I know I can't do that because I can't always be the perfect man you want me to be!!

All I need for your to do is fast forward to whenever you're comfortable... and tell me you love me again and I'll go from there...

No she said... Just fast forward the clock to 5 seconds cause that's how much time you have left... You didn't spend all your time with me wisely... And you damn sho aint take these last 5 seconds to spill your heart...

I'm sorry... But your life is about to change in 5,4,3,2,1

If you want to be a Millionaire, you gotta get up off your ass and work like one.

Shoes in Reality

It's like it got a heartbeat, its all life in the shoes/Got folks around the world worshipping them brands like Jews/

People got different styles the way they compare and contrast/

They compare their styles to the best look and contrast for the trash/

For the niggas that don't mind to spend good bread on your shawty/I think it's safe for me to invite Kimora Lee's Baby Phat to the party/

At the party I seen the DJ entertaining folks as the one man band/Rocking his head up and down, while he rocked them fresh Timberlands/

My eyesight translated from Timberlands to a different brand/

Seen skateboarders at the party kick pushing into them ice cream Vans/

Whoever said that the party invited the young bloods?/

Got immature teens making a mess with they lame ass Mudds/

But I refuse to clean that mess up, I'm all VIP/

I'll ban all you young folks like Vick's shoes in the football league/

Oh I guess they heard me, they all talking they shit/So I took off my Ralph Lauren and whooped all them bad jits/

Getting back into my zone while the party was jamming off the old school magic/My cousin brought some better music with the Reebok Classics/

Cousin brought all the old joints so the people could hear it/

But not as old as the folks when they wearing them sold out Easy Sprints/

He also brought his girl in which he used to always chump her/

So I brought my pair of love and gave her the Strictly Comfort/

But the bitch didn't want to have my Strictly Comfort and told me to leave her be/Well I guess I'll get my sisters to check that attitude of yours like Nike/

As I walked off I still hear the DJ bring the old funk back/

Like Shaq shoes that used to be hot, and some played out T-Macs/

The music progressively updated to some Ying Yang saltshaker/

I dance with my future wife, changed her last name and named my future child Liz Baker/

I dreamed while I was dancing that my child dated a thug/She bout his behind to my house, and I threw that little bastard out with his dirty ass Lugz/

Snapping out of the dream as the party grew over, the chick stared in my eyes at me like "I've got to have'em"/

I knew she wanted it so I asked for her name...and quickly she responded "I'm your brand new chick, and oh yeah my name is Stacy Adams"/

People can talk about how you're weird, but deep down inside they admire your courage because you're doing what they wish they had balls to do.

Bought the Man as My Daddy

Picture this, a lil black child grown up with a blind sight/

with one mother & no pappy cause da lil child increased da man's fright/

Since the fright, mother & pappy always used to fight/

So one winter he came in da room one last time to tell da boy goodnight/

Da old folks was the only advantages in his life/

For him to grab on to so he could travel through life right/

Mother barely making ends meet, but a man stepped in to bright-
ened up da lights/
& taught da lil boy not to fall off da bike/

Even if he does fall down in different situations of life/

he told'em it's okay to cry sometimes whenever things start to get
too tight/

Well since he taught me all that, I better raise up the price/

I'm walking around with a pocket full of money, & I don't wanna
spend it on ice/

But I was hungry in all areas before, should I spend it on red
beans & rice?/
or maybe spend my money on a man with advice?/

Or should I spend it on someone very polite?/

Enough questioning myself, I'm gonna put all that shit together and
buy him as my step daddy tonight/

If you ask God for something, make sure u are in the condition of all the things that comes along with it (Good or Bad) when you receive it.

American Dream

I think folks don't understand... No let me take that back... I know folks don't understand...

Cause if they understood what was going on then we wouldn't be seeing half of what America see's today...

Looking at politicians on tv today... makes me wanna laugh...

Cause these fools get paid to turn blue in the face and trick the world with all the bullshit that's coming from they mouths...

Like Bush... I'm sick of looking at your square headed face telling us lies on television that the war on terrorism is making progress...

Telling us that you love the American people but didn't care if Katrina swept away all the American colored people...

You full of lies... got caught more times lying than Barry Bonds shooting steroids, Vick denying dogs, and Clinton denying Monica...

That just shows us right there that we cannot put our faith in man... Cause everybody lie about something...

From 1968 till this day... I just wanna laugh in ya face... Cause it aint get no better...

The only thing that got better was technology... And technology is biggest weapon on earth that kills everything...

Created cell phones to reach out to more people... Which gives opportunities to reach out and break more people...

Computers to chat with long lost friends and meet new people... which makes room for more sex creatures...

Also made a lot of us cowards because 50% of all Americans say things on the computer or through a text message than they would in your face like back in the day, the old fashion way...

Martin Luther King needed to die back in 1968... Cause if he came back to life today to see the ignorant nigga with his pants below his waist...he would slap all the colored and say what the hell happen to this place...

And Malcom X would slap Michael Jackson and say "brother I used to dye my hair 2 play the white man's race and that wasn't the way... now why did you get rid of your black face?" "And why did you get rid of that big walnut nose?"

That's what you get for trying to be nosy, tryna find out what you'll look like if you changed yourself...now where ya nose now? People lose things when they become to nosy...

Can somebody hand me a broom...and get every troubled child, gang member, and every person causing disruption in this world... And make them sweep this place up...

We got dirt stains and juice stains that's stuck on our past and future that we wont ever be able to scrub up...

We got ancestors that's turning in they graves cause they great grand-kids breathing in peer pressure... And when they breathe in peer pressure... peer pressure makes' em breathe in drugs...

And then the drugs will grow from one person to another get planted by thugs...

After planted by thugs the drugs will be sold to people and then some of those people will turn into broke people...

So broke that they loss everything, now they holding up a sign full of lies saying wounded vet... Need some money...

And then the people with money in the cars will pass by and drop no money and the person with no money rob and kills everybody for some change and go to jail.... Well that's America for you...

Politics, wealth, high positions, and holy water wont save you...

Shout and cry all you want to... to free the troops overseas cause it aint happening... the world is gonna end with war...and end with people fighting people...

We are in the book of Revelations at this moment of our lives and its just a moment of time before our card will be pulled...

This thing we call life...is like a board game...Except you're actually in control of your every move without somebody moving you there... Cause God gave us free will...

God put us all in this checker game to see if we are going to jump the black pieces without thinking about your surrounding of other things in the world that could jump you and kick you out the game with death...

Because we got so many people that aint playing the game right and tryna cheat they way through the game of life thinking they wont get jumped...

That's why its gotten worse...its growing worse every day and year by year... Cause its so many distractions out there most folks don't believe that the lord is here...

So you tell me If you think the American dream...No not the American dream... if you think the world's dream is still alive...

I'll answer it for you... its not about the world...Its about you...cause the world aint thinking bout you...

You were born alone...and you gone die alone...

Its however you choose to live your life...Cause every person plays a role in what's happening in the world ALONE!!

Damn Roaches

Flipping my remote and settled on one channel and a roach pops up...

Grandma stop beating the T.V... it aint real, its a roach running across the screen...

Oh it looked kinda real...

You know we gone have to do something bout these roaches...

I'm getting sick and tired of these little bastards running round the house... Who gone go to the store and get the spray?

I will...

Then you went on and get the spray and came back...

Grandma I got the spray...

Good baby...gone head and spray the whole house and tell err body to get out of here...

Aight... err body yall gone have to get out of here so I can spray... After I'm done we can go out to eat...

And you spray the house... the whole house just greasing the cracks and windows and stuff...

9 hours later everybody back in the house... and you open the door to see the results

...You see all 135 roaches just laying on they back upsides down dead...It's like hurricane Katrina of roaches done passed by...

but of course... It's always one of somebody or something still standing and made it through war...

As I swept all the dead roaches outside... I heard a pppssttt...

Hey you... And I looked around like what the hell...

He said hey you... look down...

And it was one barely alive granddaddy roach that looked like he had been around since my grandma great grandma was living in the house...

He said look here boy...You done won da battle...but we aint loss the war cause we gone getchu nigga!!

Yeah I gotcho nigga... and I stomped on em and swept him out the house...

But what I aint kno is that this granddaddy roach was a straight up soldier...

3 days later we all eating popeyes...and my grandma asked for the kool-aid and I got up to look in the refrigerator...and when I opened it up... I saw something brown moving around in the kool-aid

And I got closer...and here is one of granddaddy nephews swimming around with a scuba diving fit on holding up a sign saying "you a dead nigga"

And you a dead roach.... And I took'em and poured his ass down the garbage disposer...

But I started to hear other noises too... this funny noise coming from the living room like the march with martin luther king...

Grandma...Them roaches back again...

Get the spray and spray them little bastards....

But the spray wasn't working...I'm spraying...they marching...I'm spraying they marching...

And I'm like... Damn... Why they aint dying?

I looked up close and discovered that these roaches came for war... They all had on spray proof vests with oxygen masks on...

Running after us like we stole something from em...

I'm hiding in the bathroom while errboy else in the room putting tiles in the cracks of the door so they wont get in...

And the granddaddy roach just knocking on the door saying... aye...I done told you we gone getchu nigga...you thought I was playing? That's what y'all black asses get for letting them bad ass little kids walk around chewing cookies and leaving open potato chip bags around...

Shit when yall eat...we don't complain...

We hungry too... Come on out...

Then grandma and the kids yelling and hollering...

And I looked back and I seen the phone and phonebook... shit I'm finna call the exterminator on yall asses...

Hello.... Yea I would like to have full service of extermination in my house...we got roaches...

Uh... how many roaches are in the house sir?

It's a whole family squad in here... just multiply all the times snoop dog got caught smoking weed by 10 and add it up...

20 mins later the man shows up and get the pump spray all over the house while hiding behind the shower curtain and grandma and the kids hanging on the ceiling fans cause the roaches broke pass the tiles in the crack....

And when it was all set and done...well I solve your problem for you... they shouldn't be back unless you have food lying around or so... and I heard another voice... and I looked down...

It's the same granddaddy still holding on barely alive saying... ppsssttt... yeah we gone be back...yal gone eventually get caught slipping...and when yall do... we gone getchu nigga!!

The right

Something so right... Can be so wrong/
  And something so wrong...... Can be so right/

How do I know that its wrong?.... Huh?

My job aint paying well enough, and its too late to find another job
  in 3 days/
  The landlord said that I got 3 days before he kick me out of
  my place/

Now its right in this situation to expand my judgment and get quick
  money and start hustling/   Aww damn, according to the sys-
  tem, and the legislation... I'm wrong. And if they catch me, here
  comes the questioning/

Man forget that, how can my rights equal out to be wrong/
  When I'm trying to do anything and everything I can to keep my
  family and me strong?/

Let me take 2 steps back in reminisce where my heart belongs/
  Turn the volume up so I can hear what going on/

I hear everyday on the television that the unemployment rate is
  going up/
  hear that every brother with dreads going in for a job interview is
  already fucked up/

Some folks with no money and never had nothing in life go in the
interview looking rough/
You can have all the things they need, but they say you aint get
the job because you wasn't dressed up/

Now how can something so right...Can be so wrong?/
And something so wrong... Be so right?/

Saying I'm wrong because I wasn't dressed up/
But I'm right cause I had the skills for the job, and your wrong
cause you don't know what the hell I been through to say that I
needed to dress up/

The last time I checked it was to look on the inside to see what
the heart holds/
And not look on the outside cause it's not always diamonds
and gold/

I guess its time for you to say that I'm wrong/
Cause now I'm 2 days away from getting evicted and my paycheck
is taking too long/

So I'm gonna go out and commit the what you call wrong and rob a
person for they lucky charms/
And I'll put all my belief and rights to ask, and sacrifice myself...
even if you end up catching me and I'll end up singing prison songs/

I'll do what I think is right and continue to disapprove your wrong/
Damn right I said it all.... Just to keep the lights on/

THE RIGHT

Now how can something so right...Can be so wrong?/
   And something so wrong...Be so right?/

It's the last night...it's the last night...it's the last night for me to get
   my shit right/
   I guess its time to disobey what you call wrong.... I guess I will
   never see what you see... I never could see Christ/

In my mind I'm right/
   so I hopped my right ass in the car... And drove up the 711 and
   took the clerks life/

I felt I was right... No good paying job, Paycheck wasn't coming
   through soon/
   The only right thing to do was to rob and steal from you/

Lost my life/
   Lost my sight/
   Lost my everything because I was right/

The ones that said I was wrong in the 1ˢᵗ place (the police) came in
   took my life/
   And the money that I stole couldn't get to the landlord that night/

The wrongs knocking on my apartment door waking up my wife/
   And told her that your husband aint coming home tonight/

She found out...... that I lost my life/
   All because...... I knew I was right/

Landlord still didn't give a damn if I loss my life/

And told my kids and wife... I'm sorry... No money... No nothing... You all have to leave tonight/

Now how can something so right...Can be so wrong?/
And something so wrong...Be so right?/

We all think we right? Right?/
You call them wrong when they think they right.... And they call you wrong when you know your right/

I must rest the case and speak for us all and say fuck the wrong... It's all about the right.

I almost failed every grade from 5th-12th, not because I wasn't smart... I just wasn't motivated. It even carried on to College, which I served 1 Semester and dropped out... Not to forget I possessed 15 Jobs since age 13. I always knew I would be something, I just didn't know WHAT or HOW it would happen... Inches away from joining the Navy at age 19, being fired from Wal-Mart at 20 & walking out on 1 of my favorite Jobs (working with incarcerated youths) at age 22 to chase this thing called a DREAM not knowing where I was gonna get my next dollar... Went home, got on my knees & prayed to God and he said "Just apply #FCHW (Faith, Consistency, & Hard Work) & I will take care of you"... 1 year later, after 4 years of Entertainment... I am proud to say that I am a highly blessed 23yr old... The biggest & youngest Entertainer coming out of my troubled hometown... 2012 car sitting outside, Family good, & inspiring Thousands! Got loads of Haters, Dick Riders, & fake smiles from people who never gave a damn about me. I'm sharing this story not for bragging rights, but to show you that God is REAL, & if you want something... No matter what ANYONE says... by all means, DO IT!

What is holding you back? What are you afraid of? Do you really wanna achieve? Are you willing to make the sacrifices?

Letter of Opportunity

As a lil boy playing football outside my house, the mailman would always come around 3 o'clock to hand me the mail...And as I took the mail, I always laid on it the counter for mamma to look at it when she got home...

And err time she came home I would watch her keep the bills... and throw away the junk... Until one day I asked her what was inside the envelopes that she called so called junk...

She said nothing and threw more in the garbage... Then told me to take out the trash...But I envelope wasn't torn...

So later on that night I took out the trash while she was sleep and dug through all the napkins, chicken bones, and other filthy thangs because I was just that curious...

And I found it... Slid my fingers through the envelope because I was curious of what this so called junk was...

And the letter read "this is your time and your opportunity to get whatever you're looking for right now"

So I put it in my back pocket and mamma came out upset asking why I was digging through the trash collecting junk...

I said mamma this is not junk... This is my letter of opportunity... my door that could soon open if I work hard enough to find the right key...

You can think I'm crazy all you want to just because I went through the trash can... But finding an opportunity that can mold me into something one day... is worth getting your hands dirty for...

You see I realize one big thing about people... We tend to judge the book by its cover... That homeless man you tossed 3 cents to could be Jesus...

That woman that keep asking all them stupid questions could really be smart... That man that keep claiming he got cash on the outside... is really driving his broke ass around in that rented Cadillac from enterprise on the inside...

Its funny how we say we don't like something but at the end we end up liking it... Wanna mute your ears of stories that your grandfather keep telling... But when he told you to sitcho ass down & listen you got something out of it...

It's the exact same thing when it comes to junk mail... The outside says get a capital one credit card of 10,000 with 4% interest... Man this is too good to be true... Rip, tear, trash...

But you aint bother to look inside so you end up missing out on your blessing...

Err body get junk mail... And yeah the majority of it sounds too good to be true... But I know somebody who took the time to open, read, and observe...

A lil boy, born August 4th 1961 who just happened to find junk mail that read on the outside... Your black, you monkeys will never make it

But on the inside it read "this is your time and your opportunity to get whatever your looking for right now"...

And he put that letter in his back pocket... Graduated Columbia University, Harvard Law School, became the Senator of Illinois, bent them lies backwards and said... "You're black, you monkeys will never make it..."

Became the 1st Black President with all Americans saying he was the man... Returned that same letter back to them liars with a stamp of him sippin red kool-aid in his hand that said "yes we can"

So its no excuse... No excuse for you to miss out on your opportunity... Because some of you have the mail right there in front of your face and don't know it...

And some of you actually took the time to open it but don't know what to do with it...

Its no excuses... Cause since Obama proved what the world thought was impossible... I don't ever wanna hear another person saying I cant do this... Or black person saying the white man did it...

He aint do it, you did it to your self... don't put your life problems in the palms of another man...

Don't you understand? When you wake up err day you should already have that napkin tied around you neck with the fork and knife in yo pocket prepared to get that turkey...

Its not time for games... Stop allowing these people to weigh you down like heavy ankle weights...

Because they aint nothing but a big distraction and blocking your view... So if I were you I'll say forget you, chase my opportunity, and cut that boyfriend/girlfriend loose...

Cause your time is limited... you aint got all the time in the world to respond to your letter because its some people in the world that received the same letter and prepared themselves heavily making sure that they beat you to it...

So flush all the B.S. down the toilet and tell your friends/ boyfriends or girlfriends that you got business to take care of... And if they still cant seem to understand then keep flushing... Just make sure that lil piece of turd don't return after you flush...

Ad once you've mastered your steps on how to put that turkey 1st and the B.S. last... Then tie your shoes tight, pack your bags and get going... cause you got work to do...

Get Better

Sooner or later its all gone get better...It's gone get better!!

Nah!!

Let me stop lying to myself... What the hell am I lying to myself for?

It aint gone get no better in this world because its some ignorant people out there that just don't get it...

I never could understand why black people say they wanna make it out the hood but instead do things to keep'em in the hood

Why is it that folks that come from a good family background, with the father being the Deacon and your mother being the secretary of the church end up being the worst ones?

Why is it that when niggas go to jail for robbing a bitch and you still got the dummies out there saying free my nigga?

Why he need to be free?

I'm gone start stomping my feet with my eyes close til the count of 3

1......2......3....... Wake up!!!

Where the daddy at when your kids skipping school?
Where the daddy at when that behind needed to be toe up when they cutting up in school?
Where they at?

Black people wake up!!

Why mammas lie to the kids and say they daddy ran away and wasn't shit.... But deep down in reality it'll take more than Jesus to find out who they daddy is!!!

Black people wake up!!

You tell me the real reason for voting Obama in office... Why?
Cause he black?
With or without a black president we still wouldn't know how to act...

Black people wake up!!

Crazy for not at least using a condom...you aint dead yet... I don't know if you going to hell... but you'll witness your 1st burn when you piss out fire... I wish yo ass well

Black people wake up!!

Why black people always blaming the devil and the white man for they issues but wont blame they own self? May the lord be with you!! Lets hand them a tissue!!

Black people wake up!!

Who is that knocking at my door? Oh nigga you came here knocking on my door cause you wanna fight? But when Jehovah witnesses knock on the door... you aint nowhere in sight!!

Black people wake up!!

Why black people grow so impatient when church services running so slow and start humming at the pastor when they ready to go?

Black people wake up!!

And since I took it to church I might as well tell yall the funny things people do in the church.

As a little boy I used to hate going to church... and my mamma used to wake me up on Sundays and say wake up you taking yo behind to church...

Dang mamma, why we gotta go to church? And why we always gotta sit next to that old lady who always tryna hand me the stale peppermint from out that big ass purse?

Sunday school couldn't get any worse...I aint never pay attention to what they say...I was always the little bad ass in the last row of the church... picking at the lady with that James Brown wig on and the mustache across her face.

I wanna know why black pastors steal money from the church? And then front like the church need to pay off bills and say...... "If you can, church people we are asking for 2 dollars. Remember God loves a cheerful giver!!"

And why we cant shut them crying ass babies in the church!! Keep tryna shut'em with the bottle knowing that something aint right!!

And why some pastors get off topic from the word and keep making that same "haaa!" noise breathing all heavy cause they don't know what they talking bout?

And I never could understand why black people spend 100 and something dollars on clothes and stuff they want... but when its time to give God money...what he get? 1 dollar!!! Why must he get to 2nd class effort?

And why the only time we call on Jesus is when we want something or scared?

All people wake up!!

Things aint gone get not better...because as long as we keep exercising ourselves with ignorance and lack of knowledge...It wont get better!!

All people wake up!!

As far as I'm concerned its best to establish a 1 on 1 relationship with God because we cant trust no man... So stop depending on these pastors enhance your life because some of these false prophets are gone send you straight to hell!!

So what am I telling you? Got milk or got Christ?

Put both together and you'll be alright... you'll just be a strong body Christ!!

And then things are gonna get better!!!

I Come 1St

I'm not the average Joe... I'm not your average mail man... I won't always deliver you things that you want on that special day...

You see I'm a real picky guy and unlike some guys out there... I actually have standards for myself...

I follow my standards along with faith... Everyone must do that... Even in the bible it says faith without work is dead....

And I don't beg to God for a girl because begging aint the way... I'm so sick and tired of everybody begging for a man or woman...specifically females...

But what I do is pray to God for woman that I would like to have...

When I pray...I tell em "lord...I don't come to you much asking you for a woman cause you know how I am... but lord... send me an all around respected woman...

I want a black girl... don't matter if she full black as long as she got black in her... cause I love my sisters...

A girl with natural long hair like my mamma... light skin...with nice teeth and a girl that has a big juicy heart filled with humbleness...

I love a girl with a big juicy heart...Aint nothing like it... Somebody like that makes me wanna grab a straw and find the veins that's surrounding the heart and drink it till I get full...

And when I get full that means I'm satisfied because I know that I drunk from a heart that can not only share humbleness for herself... But can be shared with a man that was dehydrated from it...

You see in Phillipians 4:6 says let your request be known... so I make sure I tell god what it is that I want and need because he is the only one that I know that can provide those things to me....

So I'm walking in the store... and God put me to the test round 1...

Beautiful sister... asked for her number and took her out on the 1st date to a restaurant and she was too thugged out for me...

Lord... I'm back... I appreciate you sending me a girl and all but... Why you had to make her so aggressive?

And he said because you didn't listen to me... so I asked'em for another one...

And he said ok... And put me to the test round 2.

2nd date found this girl at blockbuster... and was looking at the romance section... So I asked her for her number and I took her out on our 1st date to a waterfall...

Waterfall is perfect...nice date with nature... but this girl loved nature a little too much... She started kissing up on me "not like I aint like it" ... and wanted to reveal the nature of her inner thighs to me within 40 mins...

And I went back to God and said "lord... I told you I wanted an all around respected girl... why you send me that garbage? You knew waste management was suppose to pick her up last Monday...

Why is that I never can get the one I'm looking for... but when you look at folks in church... Half of em are married with a family and happy as hell...

And he said because you didn't listen to me... so I asked him for another one...

And he said alright but I aint sending you no more... U better know what to do with it...

So I saw this girl at work and she was the light skinned girl with long hair and straight teeth that I had asked about...

And I spoke to her and we started vibin... And asked her for her number and said I wanted to take her out tomorrow...

And she said oh where you taking me? Seafood restaurant... Poetry club...

Don't worry bout it... Just put on the flyest outfit you can find and I'm gonna pick you up round 10 in da morning...

10 in da morning? Where we going?

Man we going to church...... Church?

Yeah church...... didn't I say in the beginning that I'm not the average Joe?

You see I just thought about it... People wonder why they relationships don't last long and I found that answer...

God gave me 3 tries to get my act together... He said I come 1st in everything you do no matter what it is... and a lot of folks forget that I'm in charge of your romance...

That's why I have so many kids without fathers and parents that cant solve they problems...

Because the lovers can tell each other that they love'em everyday... they both spend time with each other almost everyday.... And they say they miss you when they both miles away...

But I'm more than just miles away... why cant you tell me that you love me everyday? Why cant we keep a long distant relationship and tell me every now and then that you've been thinking bout me?

Why cant you hold your pillow tight and cry over me all night?

But when a man or woman gave you cards and things for the past 7 months... don't mean nothing...

I've been giving you things all your life... and you cant cry over me? You can go to the club and dance but in my house you shy of me?

Exactly... that's why I'm gonna end it between the 2 of you... because I thought you was gone claim me as your boo... I don't ask much from you...

So break up with me and leave me out of your life.... And get into a relationship and see how much hell you go through!!

Sounds Good

Tell the world what they want to hear, that's right gone head and
    tell'em/
    Get'em mixed up with emotions until the truth tells'em/

I got the new job with Cooperate America today/
    For real? "she say", well lets go out and pop some champagne
    and celebrate/

Nah child not today, I don't want to jack up my credit rate/
    I'm going to wait until my change transact to my account on the 8th/

You see the lies she telling? Why she telling it? Because it sounds good/
    Telling false statements knowing it wont get her out the hood/

The stories sound fine now, but late their misunderstood/
    And later on down the path you'll be saying you should/

It'll be to late to say what you should've done/
    The only should've done you should've did was not to create a lie
    number one/

Some folks need to step up and focus on the aftermath/
    The equation can turn out wrong if you don't review before you
    do the math/

Paparazzi's step in the stars lives and post up all the nonsense/
    They advertise the glory so the whole world can grab the hint/

The broke jokers telling they boys how they money getting spent/
  While they ladies tell they girls how they man paying they rent/

SHHHIITTT!!!

Now aint that a lying little BBIITTCCHH/
    That brother cant even cover your kids/

He got 3 kids of his own/
    And telling his boys he get paid, man that tax money been gone/

Your boys come to your crib and see eviction notices at your home/
    Also discovered the reason why you use your cell phone when
    your home/

Cause yo' broke ass couldn't afford to keep the house phone on/
    You blame it on the crackas and they saying "sorry Javon
    you're wrong"/

The false glory sounded like you was riding on the yacht/
    The world found out its bullshit, they cracking your back/

Asking you "where all your money at?"/
    you got to find a different story to cover your slack/

You cant say that your working cause you still selling crack/
    Tell them what they want to hear since you went through all of that/

Expression

Every poet is taking a risk for the things that come out their mouths

You can speak the truth or the lies, tolerance or the ignorance

We are held reliable for what we say...

I don't like the topic you talked about... O well...

    I don't like how you degrade women... O well...

    I don't like how you talk Christ one day and the next you discussing pussy... O well...

    I don't like how you talked about drugs... my cousin was hooked on drugs... O well...

    And I don't like how you talked about the little girl on the drug free commercial when she got hit by high drivers.... My son got hit by a car.... O ... Well

What do you want me to do? Take notes on all the things you don't like and apply it to the stage?

So if I take notes on the things you don't like and say something... Debra aint gone like it... then I'm gone have to take notes from Debra on what she don't like and Becky aint gone like it... Then everybody from the audience gone have something to say...

So lets rewind this and act like I took notes from the whole audience tryna' please em...

Ladies and Gentlemen give it up for J.B...

Oh how yall doing... this is my poem that I put hard work into so
bear with me...

I just blew up in the game of hip hop...

(What did I tell you bout the word blew, blow, or blown?) don't use
any substance of that word because my auntie was in the world
trade center when the building blew...

Aight I'm sorry...

Old man mind yo' own business....

I though I told you to respect yo elders... and here you are up here
talking bout us...

I'm sorry...

My teacher gave me a F in her class

Aye man... I thought me and you had a deal? That the F word had to
go... F words aint no good... Fire, fake, fuck, freak, fony!!

Aight I'm sorry... This shouldn't bother nobody

Jesus is the answer to all my problems...

Yo, yo, aye bruh... I told you not to go up there talking that Jesus
junk cause err body aint saved...

Tell Jesus to answer yo problem after the devil's beep on the answer-
ing machine cause aint no problem getting solved in here!!

Alright this is the last one...

I just discovered a roach on my kitchen counter...

I know you not talking bout roaches after I told you not too... my grandma died in a car accident when he was driving on I-4 when the roach jumped on the steering wheel and turned over 5 times and got killed...

Man you no what...... O well...

How can you expect me to express myself when I still got somebody that always got something to say?

How can I express myself?

So it it's serious.... I'll let you have it...

Take away me... Right along with the other poets, rappers, pastors...

And who would be in charge of the entertainment then?

No music, no spoken words, no voices... this world would be a dead beat.... All because err body got something to say...

So next time when you hear or see somebody spit what they wanna talk about... Just nod your head and clap yo hands even though you don't like it... and shut yo mutha fucking mouth!!

Im Gone Teach You!

At this point of my life... I done been exposed to all different kinds of people in this world and at an early age... And it aint hardly nothing that can get pass me...

But of course you know that err body is hard headed in they own lil way if somebody say they not then they lying...

So one night before da' sky turned bright... I came home, opened my door, turned on the lights and discovered I had a surprise birthday party...

But I didn't smile, they was looking for me to be happy & shocked... But I wasn't... I was only shocked of the fact that it was bout 100 hard headed people in my house...

& instead of me asking what issues they had in they lives... I already knew because I had a pair of x-ray vision contacts in my eyes that could read they hearts & minds... & I became upset...

They was even cooking dinner for me in the kitchen & I was just sitting down just thinking how I'm gone talk to these individuals bout the hard headed decisions they making in they lives...

Minutes later my cousin came up to me & asked me in front of err body... "How food smell cuz?" I said it smelled like bullshit... And the music & err body stopped...

I said don't give me dat crazy look cause err body in this place got
something they need to work on... So if somebody aint letchu
know already, just sit down and listen cuz I'm gone teach you...

How to use the remote...

I'm gone teach you... How to turn to channel 1 & use parental
control, because its gone take a lot more than using the remote to
push "parental control on" to block the porn channels from yo' 8
year old son...

Here's rule number #1... kids can grow up to be hard headed some-
times, & one of the main gadgets these days... is that computer...
Stop using "time out" cards, punishment times, slap on the risk,
brush, picks, & rulers... & yank out that belt or stick, slap'em off
the computer & say I'm the main user...

I'm gone teach you... How to turn to channel 2 & re-adjust yo' judg-
ment single mothers...   Like when fathers not around and he
sending child support checks... Scratch off "support check" and
you don't spend it on the child... You already know the rest...

I'm gone teach you...

How to turn to channel 3 & put some duct tape cross yo' mouth...
Cause instead of telling the truth, you gotta make up lies... and
sometimes don't even lie cause you trapped in a difficult time,
you just lie to lie, make up yo' own stories... & start believing
yo' own lies!

I'm gone teach you... how to push the rewind button the remote, cause rewind back to channel 1 parents & grab that lil 15 year old girl that think she grown, walking around with that mini skirt tryna get exposed...

So why don't you just hire a fake child molester to throw yo' lil girl in the backseat of the 2002 Chevy Malibu... To say whats wrong with you, you lucky I aint rape or kill you, but I bet next time I see you, you'll be wearing the right clothes & walking around with pride by keeping your legs closed...

I'm gone teach you... How to push the skip button on the remote & skip to channel 4... I don't invite or open the doors to err body in my life... You could be a stranger, better yet backstabber, no better yet a murderer...

And I see you sitting outside my door asking me can you come in... hell no, yo shoes dirty... if you wanna come in then you better wipe yo feet... Cause I don't want you coming in here with shit on the bottom of yo shoes messing up my carpet...

I'm gone teach you... How to turn to channel 5 & push da pause button on the remote, cause some of these smart educated people need pausing... Putting on dat game face at school thinking you just the smartest thing on earth cuz you pushing a 4.0...

I'm proud of you, but let me pull you out that school & throw you into what they call the "REAL WORLD" & grade you on your common sense and see if you'll even score a 2.0!

I'm gone teach you... How to push resume on channel 5 & turn to 6... Take the battery out the remote, leave it on the couch for the joker you got laying around the house... He picked up the remote, tried to turn to channel 7, & said man this is crazy... Better tell em to get off his ass, go to that TV & stop being lazy...

I'm gone teach... How to skip channel 7 & go to 8... Cause you always complaining how bad you want things but aint never attempt to try... I don't feel sorry for ya... I only respect driven people... the ones that try, sweat, and sometimes cry... So if you aint driving then I refuse to be your passenger... Get the hell out my face...

I'm gone teach you... How to turn to channel 9 and sit sum of these people down to let'em know that we cant play around with life no more...

Cause its some people that cant breath no more... eat the food we eat, chill in the nice cool A/C, have the jobs we have, and some cant even take baths... And you got the nerves to say too good to work at fast food restaurants & scrub toilets for 6.55...

I'm gone teach you... How to stay on channel 9, push pause & the rewind button just one more time... Cause I'm gone need some black people to pause & take a good look @ they own people in Ethiopia & rewind back to the past to look @ the type lifestyle our ancestors had... And you got the nerves to say you too good to work @ fast good restaurants & scrub toilets for 6.55...

So if you just that good to realize how fortunate you are... Lets start a reality show... & instead of calling this trading spouses, we gone put the people from Ethiopia & our ancestors together & trade em' on a boat for America's top unsatisfied black people & call this show "trading niggers!" Cause they'll chop the toes off just to have your spot...

I'm gone teach you... How to turn to channel 10, cause if you aint learning from this poem then ima spit it again!!

I'm gone teach you... How to turn to channel 11, this aint "All dogs go to heaven"... Go to church err Sunday, shout, kick, & praise... "Cause not all church people go to heaven"

I'm gone teach you... How to turn to channel 12... I like females, so I cant understand why these fellas willing to sacrifice they lives by doing something stupid, & spending the rest of they lives in jail with a whole bunch of males!!

I'm gone teach you... How to turn to channel 13 cause its time to stop acting like lil kids... I'm not holding yo hand or cleaning up after you... I aintcho high school custodian... So if you wanna stay as a kid then buy yo own TV cause I'm flippin off Nickelodeon!!

I'm gone teach you... How to push the power button on the remote to turn off these ghetto misses that stand in front of Chevys squatted down with they middles fingers up, females who's attitude is all jacked up, and you not being a lady if you always cuss...

I'm gone teach you how to turn to channel 14... it's that hoe Nancy Grace!! Flip!!

I'm gone teach you... How to push the power button on the re-
mote... Nah, this time turn off the TV... Cause the TV plays a big
roll on the garbage we have stored in our trunk...

BET + MTV = niggaz tryna be like plies and Young Jeezy... And
with these niggaz bein seen on BET & MTV might just =
yo daughter from channel 5 with that 4.0 on playboy cover
magazine...

Gone Feel Me

You gone feel me... you gone feel me... You gone feel these words dats comin out my mouth right now...

Welcome passengers... Please strap on yo seat belts and fly along because your pilot J.B. is gone take you for a ride of your life to da destination of powerful words...

Hello my name is J.B... and im your pilot today... I will be flying you to your destination of powerful words...

Now just to let you know that the place of powerful words may contain things that you may not wanna hear...

Such as, da truth, and correction of things that's going on in your life that you're running from and so on and so on...

But beware of the haters in that country because the powerful words of haters can make you or break you... Alright? All aboard?

Welcome 2 beautiful island of powerful words... But before I release you... I must say this...

I'm not only a pilot... I'm a poet, which means I'm a messenger, and this message gone slap you across the mouth like Rick James and make you say "I do" and get married to the truth...

1st off this island of powerful words will make you or break you like I said before... so look at da people around you and see how many are here now...

Because later on when its time 2 fly back home... Half of em gone be dead, hooked on drugs, hooked on society, and everything else... But only a small number of you gone change, make it back on this plane and be alright...

Cause this aint the country to be visiting if you came here 2 play around... Cause many of you gone step off this plane, let these folks words break you with they and leave you with no hope...

That's the haters job to do... Say some words that they know will make you mad and make your flesh erupt...

But nah you don't believe that person could be you... You saying that it cant happen to me... Because you came from a country that told you lies since you a child saying... "Sticks and stones may break my bones but words will never hurt me."

Wrong... So if words cant hurt you how can you be human? How can you punish a child and say no if you aint got no arms to swing da belt? How can you love God when he made his words for you and I to read his words to break our sins?
And yeah his words hurt, his words aint nothing but truth... The truth hurts and the truth can break you down with corrections...

And if you get mad when someone's words correct your words or action then here's some powerful words from God saying...

Whoso loveth instruction loveth knowledge: but he that hateth reproof is brutish.

THAT'S DA KING JAMES VERSION... But if you still cant comprehend that... Just know that God's words are so powerful, that he made international versions to break it down for you saying...

Whoever loves discipline loves knowledge, but he who hates correction is stupid... Yea he called you stupid...

Oh but those words still don't phase me cuz I don't believe in God... Oh yea... well let me ask you something... Are you financially stable? No, why... well here's come powerful words that a lot of cant handle... I just read the paper and they say gas going up 8.00 next week... Damn!! Gas is high!!

But some people cant read and some cant hear... which means you cant hear or read the words that are powerful... Well let me find a person dat cant read and deaf and show them that words aint the only thang that hurt...

Numbers hurt too... Err time they pass by a gas station err week they gone see the numbers 87-89-93 and right next to 87 da price gone say 2.00... And da next week its gone jump to 2.25... And add 25 cents to err week... And his eyes gone get bigger, bigger, and bigger...

Can you hear the powerful words coming out of my mouth now?

Another thing... Politicians may lay lie... But politicians don't joke... You wont pay them no attention... Err financial aid for college students getting yoked... Why? Because they see that folks between da ages 18-24 don't vote...

And black people... We all know OJ killed dat white woman... You could rewind back to "95" we all happy jumping up and down like we free slaves off the bench...

But the truth is... Err since Harriet Tubman found a way to free niggaz... we aint know how to act since!

Can you hear the powerful words coming out of my mouth now?

This is not a joking matter... for now on out every person that has a tongue and can talk... you take every word that come out they mouth seriously whether they playing or not...

Cause these folks carry words that you cannot trust... Truth or lies... Both of'em are powerful... So is there anybody out there that don't believe words are not powerful?

Ok... get your bags and hop off the plane... And get ready to hear what others gone say...
Cause these words hurt... And these words are real, and these words are powerful!!

You are a Star!!

Age 6: son whatchu wanna be when you grow up? A doctor...

I wanna be a doctor because they save lives and heal sick people

Age 8: Son watchu wanna be when you grow up? A lawyer...

I wanna be a lawyer because they help people when justice needs to
be served...

Age 11: Son watchu wanna be when you grow up?

I wanna be a basketball player... cause I like how Kobe did dat
360 in da' air and dunked on Iverson and everybody liked it... I
wanna be noticed...

So you want attention huh? Yea I want everybody to know me as
that star...

Ok well keep livin ya' dream... And it will soon come true... You be
that star...

Age 17: your son is one of the best high school basketball stars
around the state and you so proud of your boy... he been bal-
lin' since he was 11 and got accepted to college with a full
scholarship...

Im a star daddy...I told you I was gone be a star... I told you I was
gone be noticed... that's good son... I'm proud of you... You be
that star...

Daddy... Im so stared up with my bad self that all these colleges want me... All these teams... All these girls runnin' up on me... Sooner or later...Ima get money and Halle Berry gone be runnin' up on me...

Hahah, son you got a lot to learn... You my boy... You be that star.

February 23rd. ...... 2008... High school basketball finals... 12 seconds left on da clock... Down by 1... Stole the ball from the defender... Running down the court got 1 man to beat...jumped in the air and spun like Kobe Bryant doin da' 360... He's inches away from coming down and takin' home the championship... And POW!!

A bullet comes across the court and pierced the uprising star in his chest...

My boy!! My boy!! My boy is gone...

Your boy was so filled up in being a star and had his head stuck so far us his behind that he felt nobody could touch'em...

Daddy ran up 2 da' boy and put his hand on his son's chest and said... Who killed my boy? Who killed'em... My boy is gone!!

7 months later the boy laying around the house... Son, you haven't dribbled the ball or practiced in months... I thought you said you was a star?

Daddy I am a star... And I also told you I wanted err body to notice me... Well I accomplished half dat dream when I played ball and when da bullet pierced me in my chest...

Now I wanna upgrade... I'm gone make sho err body know me and know that ima star...

So watchu wanna be now?

I wanna be a rapper!! Uh, ok son... you be that star!!

3 weeks later... Daddy I quit... Why you quittin so soon son? Daddy because they say I suck... But I know I'm hot fire... Nobody wants to listen to anybody that raps unless they on tv or on da radio... I mean if jay-z or lil wayne wasn't famous nobody would pay them no mind...

Cause its so many folks doin it dat it became a lotto... You got hundreds in your neighborhood dat wanna rap, thousands in da city, million in da state, double digit millions in America, and billions worldwide...

I even rapped in front of da church and everybody looked in they bibles and started having side conversations because its so many folks tryna rap that it bores them...

So daddy I quit... I cant do this!!

Son don't quit... and Stars don't under estimate themselves... Stars keep striving for success... And you acting like a loser, you always been a loser...

Daddy you calling me a loser? You saying I've always been a loser? You told me to be that star?

Yeah exactly... I always told you 2 be that star but you never was the star... Everything you say you was gone be you went half way with it and gave up on it...

Got shot in the chest and say you wanted to upgrade and accomplished dat dream but you didn't... you stopped dribbling that ball because you was too scared to go back on that court and get die for your dream!!

You a punk, and ima keep calling you a punk cause you go half way with everything and quit!!

2 pac got shot in the studio and still came back hard as ever...Alonzo mourning had a kidney transplant and still stepped back on the court hard as ever...

Jackie Robinson was spit in the face and still swung that bat hard as ever... Michel Jordan was cut from the team in high school and came back to try outs the next year hard as ever...

Kanye was in a car accident with face swelled up, a plate in his chin and jaw sealed up and still spit through the wire hard as ever...

They are real stars... I keep telling you to be that star because you aint that star yet... And just because you got hand claps, compliments, and girls running up to you don't make you a star...

You talking that talk but you half way walk the walk... you all bark... But no bite... And since you not biting then niggaz gone assume you weak and tell you to bite on they nuts and take you as a joke...

So son, get up off your behind and you BE THAT STAR...

Daddy, I've already been off my behind... I been quittin err thang I did cause... I'm a poet... I was too shamed to tell you that!! (laughs)

A poet? Son I told you to be that star... not that falling star... Poets don't make money!! All the dreams you had, had money behind it... But poetry wont take you nowhere...

Nah daddy, that's where your wrong... Cause a poet is a prophet... And not all prophets make money... and if you a real prophet and real in anything that you do...

You would treat that dream like a love partner... Do it for love, passion, and for free... But I cant always do it for free... because some folks would take advantage of yo' dream and wear you out... Call you on your phone left and right just to fill you in on a struggling program... And that's why I charge people $10.00 for my cd's...

I wanna make sure to see if they really listening to me... but at da same time supporting me...

Cause folks don't know how hard it is to travel miles while gas is high and get da word across to them and leave with a thank you, good job, but a sell of only 2 cd's...

And this is when money become a problem... cause different poets that come through they town and they wont even pitch in a dollar for donation...

Thinking that it aint dat serious but it is that serious... Everybody that steps behind the mic or behind the television screen changes more lives than ever...

You can go to church and your pastor spreading a bad message to everybody but td jakes can spread it better.

Ricky Smily can tell you how ugly patrick mamma is in your face and you wont laugh... But behind da mic you gone laugh harder...

If he told the people in they face to sit down they would say no... but behind da mic... Sit on down sit on down... They would think smarter...

Cause if they don't think smarter than the person behind the mic has all the power and call em out and everybody would laugh at em... And nobody likes to be called out!!

Because he's behind the mix and the tv... More people listening to him and paying attention to him... Ready to be entertained... Getting that attention...

Behind something that everybody in the world today is addicted to... Its like they worship you... they listen to you and most of them would want to be like you...

So when you aint droppin at least some kinda change to da folks behind da mic and on tv and you got da money and spend it on dumb stuff that wont last you forever...you just remember that words gone always last forever...

Them old K's u just bought wont be able to be reflected and played into a cd or dvd player...

But with these words... You can always go back and pick up on what you forget and missed... So you tell me which one you rather waste your money on? Words or BS?

You wont spend it on none? Well sometimes I agree with you... you wont spend yo money on words or BS on some of these poets and rappers... because you put the BS in front of the words and come of 'em have some bullshit words coming out they mouth don't deserve nothing...

So daddy... I'm a poet... And If you don't like it then you can be that het that shot me while I was going for that dunk... A dream killer... Well an attempted-dream killer... Cause I aint letting nobody shoot me down no matter how high I jump...

Yeah I got shot down while I was up... But God called said that my time wasn't up yet... And when you thought I was dead... I was dead... I was dead for 10 mins cause God pulled my soul to the side and brought it up to heaven and said " I need to talk to you for a minute"

He said, " you are a poet my child, go out and cast the word of life and pull the peoples mind into relation "... And threw my attitude along with my soul back down to earth...

So don't size my poetry... Cause this is a lot bigger than any dream I ever lived before...

Son, you make me proud... you put up a fight for your dream, corrected me when I was need to be corrected... Showed me da game face when it was time to show it... And that is what a star is all about.... Son, you are a star!!

The Me's of My Seed

You see, awhile ago I used to think it was just me/
  was me that I needed to work on for me to proceed/

And thought in order for me to proceed I needed to believe/
  Needed to believe so I could achieve/

What was I trying to proceed, believe, and achieve for me to wake
  up out of this bad dream?/
  My bad dream was the folks that always dropped the bomb on me/

Dropping bombs so big that it followed me/
  Followed me so long that I couldn't keep my piece/

You see, I take all the negative vibe that you people feed to me/
  Say I take everything to the heart, damn right because it sticks to me/

Sticks so much, so much that is stored a seed inside of me/
  A seed that held categories of things that could break me/

You want to know why I'm saying me at the end of every line? Why? Cause
  I though it was me that was destroying me/
  thank God I cam to my senses that is was you that was provoking me/

The seed that you planted inside of me almost took the soul of me/
  started to get fertilized by bullshit and evolved into a tree/

But me, me....... I got my own pack of seeds that I planted right next
  to the bullshit chemistry/

THE ME'S OF MY SEED

The seeds that broke roots to corrupt the negative energy/

Didn't take long for it to grow into something so prodigy/
  That prodigy created a quality so strong that little kids couldn't shake that apple from the tree/

Now what that's telling me? The prodigy and quality from the tree which was planted by me/
  Allowed me to work myself through all the tribulations that you tossed me/

Allowed me to cough up the storm of humbleness and provide my story to the society/
  Provided all that just to tell them that was I knocked out cold, but now I'm on my own two feet/

Nobody cant ever tell me that I don't deserve to live so victoriously/
  Because for me living victoriously, I was running from my enemies/

I'm throwing dead end signs to all you suckers that tried to put an end to me/
  were driving so recklessly just to make me swerve down the street/

Tried to get my body drunken with a shot of Hennessey/
  Your turn being the wheel, go ahead and drive drunk... Cause you died while I was thinking of this poetry/

Written by: J.B.

Bruh You've Changed

They say bruh you've changed...

But what if I told you I'm bucking because I damn near loss my Independence because I'm Kunta Kinte in Hollywood...

You don't know the price and sacrifice it takes to be a soldier for the Lord but fight demons daily...

I gotta lotta questions that people would crucify me over like "How can gay couples raise babies?"

Ooohhh... I struck a nerve...

That boy ignorant...

You know people will be so quick to reference bullshit and get mixed in they feelings... but look in the mirror homie... How you living?

Tell me what's in your kitchen? What kinda brand you building?

You tryna say I can't light a joint and teach these children? At the same time?

Nigga you out yo mind...

Don't open your mouth if you ain't been there since day 1 on my timeline...

Most people ain't built for this game... They get a little fame, sniff cocaine... forget about God and lose they brains...

You damn right I've changed...

I'm tryna break this chain...

I'm Kunta Kinte in Hollywood... But these folks don't hear me

I got perfect situation going on... Call me Demark Vesey

It's deeper than weed, it's deeper than me...

Sometimes I gotta cuss and cutup just so niggas can see... The clear picture...

But it looks like Picasso...

Social media got these kids going coco.... And these parents are bozo...

I still care... So before you judge me saying "Bruh you've changed"... Make sure u check the shit stains in your underwear...

-Spoken

CPSIA information can be obtained at www.ICGtesting.com
Printed in the USA
LVOW12s0840230714

395547LV00003B/3/P